Tree Fall
with
Birdsong

Just as Kendall Dunkelberg's poem, "Orpheus," concludes its illumination of Eurydice being left behind in the underworld with "her face nearly restored to its former/ beauty, ... to haunt [her husband's] final days," the rest of the collection, *Tree Fall with Birdsong*, also does much to restore poetry's former beauty through hauntingly personal yet welcoming lyrics, painstakingly crafted in delightful, accessible language.

Claude Wilkinson
author of *World Without End*

The keenly attentive poems of Kendall Dunkelberg's *Tree Fall with Birdsong* reveal his long immersion in the losses and continuities of the natural world and the ways in which the other-than-human can instruct us in the pleasure and pain of being human. The magical apple tree of his childhood, with its five-grafted types of fruit, eventually grows old, and at the home of his ninety-year-old mother, the enormous maple rots and will fall. A cluster of poems near the end of the book, written during the pandemic, speaks of the both/and of earthly experience. In "Gilgamesh," "Grief is a cold dark country,/ whose citizens are clad in feathers..." But "Gilgamesh" is followed by "Inanna"—or "Ishtar, Persephone, Astarte," who brings springtime, the "soft song of her familiar doves...her bees as they collect sweet nectar." For, as Dunkelberg writes,

> ... a harvest is never an end, but a new
> stage in the cycle, the way the wild goose
> as she migrates, is always flying home,
> and the road, though it never leaves,
> always travels on, even as the river
> flows ever constant to the sea.
> ("Tessellations")

Ann Fisher-Wirth
coeditor of *Attached to the Living World: A New Ecopoetry Anthology* and author of *Paradise Is Jagged*

Tree Fall with Birdsong is a sharp-eyed meditation on the natural world and the nature of being human. Kendall Dunkelberg's beautifully crafted songs see beyond what we think we know, transforming vultures into brethren, the possessions of the dead into a smoldering treatise on grief, and cherry-picking into a familial ritual which speaks to the relentless, complicated, cyclic pleasures of life that will end, if we are lucky, in pie. These poems, full of dry humor and surprise, take on subjects as varied as love, death, cancer, lies, Gilgamesh, and even a woman tweeting in the forest—all anchored by the power and persistence of nature. With extraordinary insight, Dunkelberg considers again and again an essential question: "What is mortality in the face of this life"?

Jacqueline Allen Trimble
author of *How to Survive the Apocalypse*

Tree Fall with Birdsong

Kendall Dunkelberg

Fernwood
PRESS

Tree Fall with Birdsong
©2025 by Kendall Dunkelberg

Fernwood Press
Newberg, Oregon
www.fernwoodpress.com

All rights reserved. No part may be reproduced
for any commercial purpose by any method without
permission in writing from the copyright holder.

Printed in the United States of America

Cover and page design: Mareesa Fawver Moss
Cover art: John William Lewin (1800), courtesy National Library of Australia

ISBN 978-1-59498-160-9

For my mother

Contents

Birdsong 13
    For the Record 14
    Poem About the Economy 15
    Birdsong 16
    They Know 18
    Crow 19
    Hieroglyph 20
    If a Bird Tweets in the Forest 21
    A Different Wind 22
    December Flood 23
    Needles 24
    Beso con Lengua 25
    Burying the Bed 26
    Tessellations 28
    The Rain in Flanders 29
    The Golden Swamp Warbler 30

Cathedral 31
    Spiderwort 32
    Cancer Root 33
    Continental Divide 34
    Ghost Deer 35

Beaver Moon 36
Brethren 37
Passion Flower 38
Poem 39
Great Blue 40
Hidden 41
Cathedral 42
Patterns 43
Turning Sixty 44
Breathe 45

Tombigbee River Haiku 50
Mist on the river 51
Massive bridge girders 51
In the golden sun, men 51
Morning sun paints 52
A blue heron 52
A white egret 52
A sudden racket 53
Sign of spring swallows 53
The otter swims 53
Splash! 54
Leafless bushes 54
A pale full moon 54
Crossvine trumpets 55
Beside the fountain 55
Mayfly carcasses 55
Swallows swoop low 56
Summer still 56
A tree 56
In the dry ravine 57
Three loud kingfishers 57
One leaf twirls 57

Coevolution 58
Windswept Cave 59
La Llamada (The Call) 60
Avalon and Ingomar 61
Apple Trees 62
Protozoan Transmogrification 63

- Tree Fall ... 64
  - Windfall ... 65
  - North Star ... 66
  - The Orchard ... 67
  - Deep Freeze ... 68
  - Birthday ... 69
  - Tending Eden ... 70
  - Picking Cherries ... 71
  - Apple Butter ... 72
  - The Big Maple ... 73
  - The Rope ... 74
  - Sapling ... 75
  - A Storm ... 76
  - A Necessary Lie ... 77
  - The Stump ... 78
  - Moon Dog ... 79
- Quarantine ... 80
  - Black Racer ... 81
  - Ash Wednesday ... 82
  - Quarantine ... 83
  - Stereoscopic ... 84
  - Partial Eclipse ... 85
  - Zero Gravity ... 86
  - Nightshade ... 87
  - Gilgamesh ... 88
  - Inanna ... 89
  - Orpheus ... 90
  - Eurydice ... 91
  - Osiris ... 92
  - Isis ... 93
  - In the Beginning, ... 94
- Acknowledgments ... 95
- Title Index ... 97
- First Line Index ... 101

Birdsong

For the Record

When the eye of a cormorant winks at you
across a salt marsh fringed with cane and hyacinth,
as the giant winged shadow lifts itself, scattering
a spray of murky water into a steel gray sky
over the Florida panhandle, you must stop
what you are doing, whether that is rowing
a rented boat, driving the coastal highway, or
daydreaming in a vortex of shadow.

After years in the land of darkness, the sun,
a cool silver disk, rises slowly to the surface
of a lake, shudders in the dawn of primal dew.
If you want, you can hold it in your hand,
hold it to your lips, and blow. Quick, make a wish
like on the dry seed of the dandelion. Light will shatter,
casting shards of broad leafy green and golden
sunrises tomorrow and for many days thereafter.

Poem About the Economy

Gold coins hang from branches, mist glistening
on buds about to burst into springtime currency
to be spent by doves and pigeons, while we stay
depressed about banks that have failed, revealing
the true national treasury is not in the fields, plowed
and sterilized with herbicides, but in the ditches
and fence rows, where scrub trees and bushes
sprout tender leaves like true entrepreneurs.

Birdsong

The magpie gathers all
that sparkles. He is a thief
or a garbage man.
He speaks to everything
in its own tongue.

Why, when the heron
flies, does he let his feet
dangle below his wide,
graceful wings? Is it to
keep his balance, to steer
like a ship, or could it be
the heron loves to feel
the air rush deliciously
between his toes?

I could try to write of the flickers,
but I never saw more than one
of their maple-colored tails
fanned out in flight. You saw two
of them, a couple, lit on the trunk
of a tree, their heads bobbing
in unison, both searching for food.

◊

This spring I see two brown thrashers
flying together as one ball of feathers,
a creature with four wings and two
tails in constant motion for a moment
until they break apart, and I discern
the female as one distinct bird,
the male close behind, pestering.
Now I see them one at a time
flitting in and out of the camellia,
one on guard as the other broods.

They Know

The cows know. Standing still
in the pasture, chewing cud
and steadily swishing flies.
With those enormous eyes,
they look for all the world
as if they know.

The wind knows.
It whispers to the grass.
The grass tells the trees
who pass it on to the birds.
The crickets discover it
all on their own.

But you and I, we don't.
Though on a day like today
when the sun is bright
and the cattails let loose
a flurry of tiny parachutes,
we sense there's something
the world knows.

The dogs would tell us
if only we would listen.

Crow

Would I were a crow, a dark
contrast to all around, a black
shadow in the sky that casts
deeper shadows on the ground.

Would that I could fly
over rivers and over fields,
searching for corn or a tree
to roost in or just because I can.

No one is more self-assured.
No creature more composed.
When I would speak, no one
would dare misunderstand.

Hieroglyph

How can I say in words what my body,
sitting next to yours, already knows?
Can I describe your eyes as almonds
like in those paintings in the pyramids
or lotuses, dark pools in which to swim?
Shall I call your neck a tower, your
skin dark and fragrant as cedar?
Where will I find the red of your sweater
or the words for your carnelian presence
beside me after too long an absence?
Your hands, hushed like the folded wings
of a dove, form their own language
when they fly up in answer.

If a Bird Tweets in the Forest

and there is no other bird to hear it,
or if a woman tweets where there is
no cell tower or satellite, no social
network, no Wi-Fi, will she make a sound?
Will she be the creator of the waves
of leaves around her as she walks
beyond the path, or will the wind
whirl the world around her feet?

Yet when a bird warbles in the woods,
aren't there always other birds to hear?

A Different Wind

Is it a different wind that blows
in the fall, or is it that the leaves
are dry, not full of life as they are
in the soft spring breeze?

I've been told you can't fly a kite
in the fall because the cold winds
sweep down from the clouds
and won't provide enough lift.

Yet I see turkey buzzards soaring
nearly motionless on the updraft.
They have learned the art
of navigating in the cold.

If only I could soar with them
and find my wings on these
chilly drafts or learn to fly
to where the wind is warm.

December Flood

The murky river surrounds
the town's lonely Christmas tree,
its lights still ablaze

on the peninsula in the park,
which is an island now
but soon will be submerged.

The flood invades the trees
with brilliant water but will leave
dark sludge behind, where

hundreds of dying fish will flash
silver on black banks, and golden
flowers will grow in spring.

Needles

I've tried to edit you out. After writing you down
in poems or half-poems, I scratched through the lines,
tore out the pages, not violently but with careful
consideration the way I took out the Christmas tree,
that other symbol of a midwinter celebration of light.
I packed the balls in tissue, wound up the strings
of colored lights, and placed the star back in its box.
The tree itself I removed from the stand, then drug
carefully to the curb. I vacuumed and vacuumed,
hunting every last needle, yet I know come August
I will still step on one last fragrant, dry reminder.
So it is with you, though I have expiated all
of our brief, bright flash of a past, now and then
I'm still pierced with a faint pin prick of memory.

Beso con Lengua

Back when I lived in Chicago and still ate meat,
my roommates and I loved to go to taquerias,
where you could get real barrio food, not the
Americanized fare that passes for Mexican
in Mississippi. Yet my roommates never
dared to try my favorite: *tacos con lengua*,
a cross-cultural glossolalia wrapped in tortilla.

Tongue wasn't so foreign to me. My mother grew up
eating it on the farm and passed it on to us, buying
gigantic beef tongues, studding them with cloves,
and boiling them in her biggest stock pot. We loved
to eat it hot with horseradish or cold in a sandwich,
the sensation of the cow's big, tender taste buds
on our own was our favorite part, a culinary French kiss
long before we became aware of the opposite sex.

Still, now that I've moved to the South, I'm glad
I've become a vegetarian. I don't have to draw
the line at chitterlings: somehow, intestine on intestine
doesn't have quite the allure of tongue touching tongue.
And I really have no desire to suck the flesh from
between the toes of a pig, pickled or otherwise.

Yet I have to admire the honesty of using
every part of the animal you eat, in the way
that as a boy I admired the idea of the Get Smart
Sandwich at the drive-in in Belle Plaine, Iowa,
but never could quite stomach the reality
of scrambled brains on a sesame bun.

Burying the Bed

After Great Aunt Ruth's funeral,
Uncle T hooked a bucket on the tractor
and dug a pit back of the house.

Everything the family didn't want
or hadn't claimed, he carried through her kitchen
and piled in the hole.

Pots, pans, cast iron skillets,
photo albums, his father's suits
that his mother had saved,

their old TV and La-Z-Boy,
rugs, end tables, tax forms, reproductions
of oil paintings, slippers,

even the kitchen table
and chairs, and finally their old
iron bed with the mattress

and box springs still on, floating
atop the detritus of their lives
like a toy boat tossed on the waves.

No one wanted this reminder
of their own generation, no one
was willing to sell it either.

Instead he dowsed the pile with gasoline,
tossed on a lit book of matches and watched
the history of the farm go up in flames.

When the wind picked up, the fire
nearly leapt to the house, until he ran to the tractor
and pushed the mound of dirt over

the scorched grass, then as the bed still smoldered,
filled in the pit, crisscrossing the smoking
ground to tamp it down.

The next morning nothing was left
except an unnatural rise, like a giant grave,
black and still smoking in the yard.

Tessellations
for Tessa

In the dark of winter, along frozen canals
and bridges, a flash of summer sunlight once
planted a seed, a child's head pushing into
the world the way a green shoot emerges
from a bulb, a baby forms her first clear
vowel, or a crocus bursts through snow.

Who then could predict the ripe fruit,
dark as the sweetest, tartest cherry,
the grace of the lithe otter in the Lys
as it dives to chase a minnow, the symmetry
of Escher's geese as they cross and recross
a winter sky, and the strength of the square
cobblestone planted in a Flemish high road.

Before us in a field of wheat or barley
stands a woman, her back to the rising sun,
preparing for the harvest. Her smile is the blue
flash of steel on the blade of her scythe,
yet no matter what she reaps, gathers,
and carts to the mill, some grain will scatter:
wild seed to plant a new crop of dreams.

For a harvest is never an end but a new
stage in the cycle, the way the wild goose
as she migrates is always flying home,
and the road, though it never leaves,
always travels on, even as the river
flows ever constant to the sea.

The Rain in Flanders

falls like dark hair across a shoulder,
like the poplars that sway slightly
as a peewit cries its mournful cry
and I walk alone along the Lys.
Winter only now merges into spring.
The eel fishers sit for hours
under their black umbrellas with
half-full buckets at their sides.
Their patience inspires my reveries.
The gray skies of Flanders match
my mood. Here there are no streets
filled with cars and busses, no markets
or airplanes, no desire or longing,
no love, fulfilled or otherwise.
There is no hunger, no sun, no
night, no yesterday or tomorrow.
There is only the ever-present mist,
the grass, a plowed field, and a few trees.
There is the damp air as it enters
my lungs and a cool puff of mist
as it leaves. Nothing more is necessary.

The Golden Swamp Warbler

is officially known as the prothonotary warbler,
named after the yellow-hooded Catholic scribes
of another era no one recognizes today.

Saddled with an unwieldy name, the bird is
hardly religious, yet we see them on Easter
weekend at Noxubee Refuge, yellow

egg-shaped birds flitting between cypress,
and later at the picnic grounds, we hear their warbling
high in the pines above loud, brightly colored

townsfolk, who take free canoes and kayaks
out on Bluff Lake. My son and I join them
for an hour of warm spring sun on cool water.

Clumps of cypress, lily pads, and reeds rise
from the shallow lake, where we spot
a pair of tricolored herons, several

white egrets, and then one lone golden
swamp warbler who lights on a bare
dead tree trunk inches from our gaze.

We drift close as quietly as we can and admire
this bright gift of color, until this splash of gold
against the blue of lake and sky flashes away.

Cathedral

Spiderwort

for Kathryn

Roots burrow in the dark, tunneling through clay,
pushing, prodding to explore and blindly build a web
in earth. Silken breath adheres to every grain of dirt,
tendrils split stone, reach water, draw life by osmosis
through soil, pulling it higher till from the remnants
of last year's stem a thin, pale green shoot emerges
when sun warms winter's chill, and the shoot thickens
to form a stalk along which emerge long grasslike leaves,
rough and firm, where in the crooks of each haulm
a single purple blossom unfolds around a yellow star,
the way the soul emerges after death as energy
or memory, grief, passionate longing, or relief
of those who remain to discover this stark beauty.

Cancer Root

The tumor takes root, like a seed germinating beneath
the soil, unnoticed and cryptic until it sprouts, yet unlike
the seed, does not issue life but destruction to the organism.
It breeds aberrance and becomes a black hole feeding
on the matter, the hope, the life, the energies around it.

So unlike the unassuming white flower that bears its name,
a quiet beauty, parasitic, yes, but hardly fatal, a sign of spring
and of renewal, a hopeful blossom nourished by the roots
of sunflower or burdock, prefiguring their showy blooms,
yet marked, like Cain, by an inescapable name.

The flower, when uncovered in a meadow or wood,
is a revelation; the tumor, when discovered in the tissue
of breast or liver or bone, is a sentence, now not always
to death but to a new life of treatment, a new label
of survivor for however long that term will last.

Continental Divide

Route 52 near Hibbing, Minnesota

If a drop of rain would fall,
where would it travel?
To the west of this spot
it would flow to icy Hudson Bay;
half an inch further south takes
it to the balmy Gulf; a hair
to the east and it would flow
down into Lake Superior.

We are not like that raindrop.
We travel over the divide here
in Minnesota without a thought.
It is barely a rise with only
a marker to tell we've crossed
from one watershed to another,
our fluidity so much greater and
less consequential than water.

For of course the sign is wrong.
If one drop of water were to fall,
it would soak into the ground,
traveling down to join the aquifer or up
the roots and stem of a prairie flower.
It would take a million drops, a
downpour to flow in all directions,
wearing the continent away here
and extending it at the sea.

Ghost Deer

Driving home from Meridian late at night,
we begin to see deer in the pitch-dark ditches,
first one lone doe looking longingly at the road,
then a pair, and soon whole deer families,
ghostly in the dim white refracted light
of the headlight's beam. Their eyes gleam
green, always seeming to look right at us,
though some are bending down to graze.

We are thankful to see them and more
thankful that they hold to their positions
in the ditches. In our mind's eye, we witness
the carnage that would happen if they bolted,
knowing we would end up among the wreckage.
These ghost deer silently graze, silently
bide their time, observing an uneasy truce.

Beaver Moon

As the sun spills blood
across the western hills,
the full moon slowly rises
from behind a dark cloud.
This is no Hunter's moon.
Instead, orange and round
as a pumpkin, its light
blesses the animals.

May the turkey and the deer
discover the hunter's blinds
and escape to breed again.
May the beaver and the fox,
even the coyote, find a home
out of the cold, may the bear
find a cave befitting its long
winter sleep, and may you
and I, my love, find our own
shelter to keep us warm.

Brethren

A kettle of black vultures
circle above the woods.
One settles on a branch
above me, his gray cowl
a menace, as three more
startle from the trees, their
wingtips flashing white,
their cycle widening.

There is no carrion here
that I can see, only blue
sky behind alien bodies
graceful in flight yet
awkward at rest. With one
dark eye, he looks down at me
before rejoining his brethren.

Passion Flower

No, this is not a crucifix
but a whorl of purple fragrance,
a noxious vine that suddenly
bursts into color. It is a surprise
in early summer: the only hint
of suffering is its violet robe,
not the cruciform pistil,
a yellow eye forever open.

Poem

The water in this stream
makes its own poem
without words, flowing
over rocks, its sound and
the light glancing off
ripples and eddies, more
beautiful than language.

Great Blue

Be like the great blue heron
who stands near the bank of the river.
He lets the cold rain roll off his back,
lets the muddy river flow past his feet.
When the time is right, he fishes.
When he is ready, he will spread
his great silver wings, stretch out
his slender neck, and fly away.
Until then, he waits, both within
and outside of this world.

Hidden

Winter is the season when hidden beauty
is revealed: green clumps of mistletoe
suspended in the highest branches
or squirrel nests, the palest ghost
of green lichen on fallen twigs, spiky
sweet gum balls that litter the path,
and the pearl white berries of a lone
dogwood. Soon spring flowers
will distract our eye, and in summer
a dark green mantel of leaves will cloak
trees and bushes. In fall, bright reds
and yellows in golden sunlight
vie for our attention. But on a gray
morning in January, these seed pods
and parasites sustain us. Green moss
and orange fungus on trunks bring
some warmth and color to the sharp
contrasts of bare black branches
impaled on the cold slate sky.

Cathedral

After the night of heavy storms
along the swollen creek banks,
cypress knees wave peace signs
at the universe. The sun dawns
calm and yellow, as water runs off
in rivulets, surveying the land.

But for a few downed limbs,
it would be hard not to imagine
that last night's winds and sheets
of rain were a dream, a childish
nightmare, hard not to believe in
the promise of the tooth fairy, that
out of pain comes something good.

Listen to the birds in the trees:
you cannot see them, but believe
their song. Look at the early sun
falling through cathedral arches
of trunks and branches. Feel
a gentle breeze caress your cheek.

Patterns

This stone holds the pattern
of fossilized fern, its amber
leaflets still recognizable after
eons, though the rock has been
crushed and cemented in the path
where now an orange and green,
nearly black, box turtle ambles
across, as yesterday an antlered
young buck crossed the river, a black
lab hard on its heels as he swam
to the other bank then ran
along it, headed back, but turned tail
afraid of the dog who wagged
much like the ponytail of the blond
jogger that flips in front of me and
is followed by an old man
whose indigo tattoo waves
on his arm, a sign of his war,
the way the fern must have
waved in its wind or the buck
tossed his antlers before rising
out of the water, safe on his side
of the river for now. What
is mortality in the face
of this life, stretching for ages
along a path, both future and past,
and what are our fantasies
of immortality, when daily
the patterns are reenacted?

Turning Sixty

This morning, a summer
tanager lights on a branch
before me, gracing the world
with her yellow presence,
the color of the early sun
through leaves that are only
beginning to think of change.
Soon she will migrate south
while I remain. I walk on
beside rapids in the creek
flowing over rippled limestone
as it has since long before
the road above was built or
I, or any humans, arrived.

Breathe

for Bill in the late stages of ALS

1)

feel the air
thin and clear or
thick and humid
hot, dry, cold, or sharp
feel the air drawn in
through mouth or nose
silently or snoring
calmly or hiccuping,
feel air
with each breath
a life
each life
an exchange
of oxygen and
carbon dioxide,
this breath is easy
and has been
for nearly fifty
years, each breath
so normal, so
(in)consequential
sequentially drawing
in of air slowly
or in gasps
carries your life
without struggle

but for Bill
each wheeze
of the BiPAP

machine
regular and forced
through clear
plastic tube
and mask each
breath, a life
each life, a breath
feel the air
thin and clear
thick, humid, dry
cold or sharp
feel

breathe

feel

life

2)

water
flows in hollows
finding every crevice
swirling to pool
and form new streams
that flow
into marshes
this spring so wet
and cold, the earth
shows its aspiration
the water cycle
sun on green
and mud

water flows
in hollow and morass
the earth's
respiration
renews
in gurgle and glob
this life

in the body
blood circulates
through hollow
arteries, capillaries
and veins, red
white and blue blood
as long as the heart
still pumps
electric flashes
circulate through nerves
short circuit
in arms, legs, lips
tongue, esophagus
and diaphragm
no longer pump
and thrill
on their own
to the joy of work
or sleep
the pulsing
cycles of life

3)

hear the air
flat or round

calm or harsh in
words of love
or anger
roll effortlessly
off the tongue
but for Bill
every word
a shape carved
in air, captured
with a gasp and
the uncooperative
scythe and plow of
iron lips and tongue
each breath
a word, each
word, a life

in light
in the sun
bathing the farm
warming the earth
and cows
glancing off
the water in
the pond he built
with the tractor
the geese have flown
yet the wild goose
returns
every morning
in bright sun
or rain
the pear tree

bursts into blossom
into dream
where every word
is a prayer
rolling off the tongue
an effortless
chant, a song,
a hymn
to life
to light
to the air

feel it
dry or humid
icy or searing hot
feel every breath
to never forget
this gift

Tombigbee River Haiku

Mist on the river
    shifts in swirls.
  Migrating birdcalls.

≈

        Massive bridge girders:
          morning light molts
           shimmering reflections.

≈

  In the golden sun, men
    clear brush with chain saws—
      the day remains intact.

Morning sun paints
   green treetops orange—
     autumn on high limbs.

≈

A blue heron
   skims its own reflection.
     Below, fish scatter.

≈

A white egret
   stands stock still:
     a frozen breath.

A sudden racket:
    two red-breasted mergansers
        fly the quiet creek.

≈

Sign of spring swallows—
mud nests hanging
    from bridge pillars.

≈

The otter swims,
    then dives.
    Will his wake resume?

Splash!
    The size of the fish
    grows with the ripples.

≈

        Leafless bushes:
           from the bluff, a view
           of the winter river.

≈

A pale full moon
    floats over silver fog:
   frost and first crocus.

Crossvine trumpets
   litter the path—
signs of night rain.

≈

                          Beside the fountain
                               one lost
                               baby slipper.

≈

                Mayfly carcasses
        scattered around the lamppost:
                    moon dog in daylight.

Swallows swoop low
    over grassy fields at dusk—
poor insects.

≈

        Summer still
        walks the autumn path:
           husk of cicada.

≈

A tree
falls across the path:
    bird calls.

In the dry ravine
    one day's splash of color:
cardinal flower.

≈

Three loud kingfishers
    crack open the shell
      of morning silence.

≈

One leaf twirls
onto frost-covered leaves:
    river mist rises.

Coevolution

Four artists in six paintings

Windswept Cave

after Eugenia Summer

A mountain or mesa or cliff
    with windswept sunset colors,
        or is it sunrise?
        Can you tell from the blue of the sky or the sea—
            a window in air, the dark
shadows of a cave, a foreboding night,
        or the warm embrace
of shelter
        from the stark white walls of stone
        beneath green blankets of grass,
            chaos and calm,
            blood, storm, birth?

La Llamada (The Call)

after Remedios Varo

In the courtyard of stone caryatids,
    one figure comes to life,
a woman bathed in gold starshine, her robes
    emanating incense and light,
her face, the face of the Madonna,
    her hair, wild orange-red,
a swirling umbilicus still tied
    to the evening star, Venus,
high in the dark sky above
    this massive courtyard
where women's figures emerge
    from limestone walls
surrounding her, yearning for
    her freedom and life.

Avalon and Ingomar

after Valerie Jaudon

Light glances off
the crosspieces
of a lattice or trellis,
gateway or arch,
the entrance
to a bronze world
or prison of silver
interlacing patterns
welcome or forbid,
round arches, sharp
corners clamor,
rise, and die.

Celtic crosses, vines
of silver, a labyrinth,
an ocean woven
in tapestry, cross-stitch,
braid, myriad eyes
or vulvae, exes and ohs
form a novitiate's cell,
a basket or castle,
thistle or vessel,
bower or cloister.

Apple Trees

after Mary Evelyn Stringer

Here in the orchard
   under the shade of
      intertwining branches,
light is the fruit,
   the sweet crunch of flesh
in the curve of trunk and limb,
   the air is red, gold
      and green delicious
the earth and sky
   weave leaf and stem,
twilight peace descends,
   or daybreak wafts perfume
Götterdämmerung or maiden dawn
   gloaming, aurora.

Protozoan Transmogrification

after Eugenia Summer

Even in the darkness, there is color
    microscopic, cellular, the catalyst
of change, psychotropic, psychedelic
    nuclei of books and plants
shellfish, ova, magic-
    school-bus spaceships,
libraries of vascular tissue,
    art galleries of tulip fields
    or caterpillars and trilobites,
centipedes, stars, and suns.
    Once the transmogrification
begins at the protozoan level,
    there is no stopping
its proliferation
    in music, waves of rhythm,
    reds, greens, yellows, blues,
flesh pink, searing white—
    an inner world blossoms.

Tree Fall

Windfall

Half the North Star cherry blew down in an autumn storm,
so after the last bumper crop of apples was harvested,
Mom had both trees cut: one too damaged to survive,
the other too fertile and healthy for her, at eighty-nine, to manage.

These were the last of a long line of fruit trees in our yard.
When we were young, we climbed the low branches of a magical
five-variety apple which grew Golden Delicious, Granny Smith,
Haralred, and two other reds I've forgotten, each grafted

to the same gnarled trunk, each bearing fruit in its own season,
each with its own color and flavor, its own tart crisp flesh and
tender or waxy skin, its flesh light green or pale yellow with pink
veins running to the core with its dark and bitter seeds.

North Star

The North Star was a deep red, tart pie cherry.
Its juice would stain your hands like blood, its pies
and jams preserved the richest nights and most
brilliant suns of summer for the darkest winter months.

Its companion in my childhood was the Meteor,
a bright red cherry with amber flesh whose sour
juice would turn fingers black when we pitted them.
Both trees lost limbs, eventually split at the graft

and died like the peach and apricot, which never
bore much fruit thanks to Iowa's cold winters, but
the rare, undersized orange bursts of exotic flesh
were all the more magical for their scarcity.

The Orchard

Each tree we lost in the orchard would be replaced
with a new variety. A plum replaced the apricot
and yielded a better harvest; another single apple
was planted after the five-varieties had each been lost,

and once us kids began to fly the coop, the fruit
trees gradually succumbed to a crab apple or
mountain ash, feeding birds a higher priority with
fewer human mouths to feed and hands to pick.

Yet Mom always had a North Star and always kept
a Red Rome or McIntosh through many replantings,
her pies and jam or apple butter, staples in summer, their
deep brown or dark red sauce our lifeblood through winter.

Deep Freeze

Now that part of the yard is barer, only the grape vines
remain, along with two types of rhubarb low to the ground,
the garden has shrunk to a few herbs, lettuce, and asparagus,
and the orchard is relegated to the deep freeze of memory,

where I still use the push mower under the lowest branches,
trying not to let them catch my head and arms,
or I climb the sticky limbs of the cherry, sap oozing
from the crooks in the places the storm will break,

where I am still caught like a grackle in the netting
straining for the alluring red fruit, too tempting to
leave alone, too bright and sweet to let the humans
have all to themselves, despite their deadly snare.

Birthday

As I recall, my imaginary friend's name was John.
We used to play out under the apricot and cherry
trees in the back yard, when I was three or four.
So how was my mother to know, when I asked
if I could go to his birthday party, that I would walk
three quarters of a mile to Washington Elementary
before I realized I had no earthly idea where he lived.

My parents found me, sitting on the curb
at Seventh and Main, unsure whether to cross
on the red or on the green, hoping someone
would come to bring me home. I realize now
I must have crossed that same light, confidently,
on the way to the imagined party, but I don't know
whether the cars on the highway stopped for me
or whether I was lucky enough to cross on green.

Tending Eden

The low-hanging boughs of the dwarf apricot
and cherry are treacherous for young boys
struggling with the push mower, trying
to get the whirling reel of blades as close
as possible to each stout trunk under
branches with rough bark and elbows
nearly as sharp as the barberry's thorns
that tattoo arms and legs with scratches
that last for weeks. Yet the shade
of the orchard on a scorching summer day
and the low branches made these the first
trees we could climb.
                         Here there are no
serpents, the fruit, though not forbidden,
is every bit as luscious as Eden's,
and knowledge of the other—the sticky
sap, the glossy leaves, the deeply colored,
saftig, blood-red flesh, the hard and bitter pit—
is only a hint, a premonition of adulthood.
The innocence of childhood is a lie or
a promise yet to be fulfilled, and banishment
is only temporary: being called in for dinner
or exhorted back into the sweaty summer lawn
to finish mowing.

Picking Cherries

Late June brings a certain warmth in Iowa.
Cool morning gives way to the blue sky and sun.
We don old shirts and cutoffs to pick cherries
before the robins and grackles take them all.

We unpin clothespins and struggle with the thin
black netting, tangled in twigs and leaves
caught on the rough bark of the older branches,
and we pray we don't find the carcass of a bird

trapped in the net. We then cut loose the malodorous
fly traps my mother makes: vinegar and banana peel
in a dish soap bottle, now one black squirming mass,
hung by a length of her old nylons in the branches.

Finally, we set up the wooden ladder and begin to fill
white ice cream buckets and Cool Whip containers
with the ripe fruit. Once I was the boy in the branches.
Now my wife and son pick with me from the ground.

Later we gather on the patio with my mother and bowls
of cherries and pans to pit them in. The red juice
stains our clothes and fingers until we are tired and
nearly sick of cherries. But tonight, there will be pie.

Apple Butter

Take the windfalls, the bruised yet edible
apples, and boil until soft. What I remember
about making it is the canning sieve: first
the old-fashioned kind, a cone and cone-shaped
wooden pestle used to press the soft flesh
leaving skins and seeds behind; later, a modern
one with a mesh bottom and flat metal
blade you turned with a crank; and the smell,
like vomit, the sour-sweet-bitter stench
of too many apples, and the lesson:
with enough sugar, clove, and cinnamon,
with enough cooking down, nothing
is useless or wasted. This damaged fruit
will soon be canned in jars, a dark brown
lusciousness, not jam, not jelly, nor anything
remotely resembling butter, yet priceless.

The Big Maple

We believe a tree must live forever.
It has been there all our lives, this big
maple stretching its limbs and casting shade
over our childhood and deep into the past.

It was there when our parents picked out the lot,
already a giant maple in the midst of a cornfield.
A few houses dotted the corners of Eighth Street,
but here on what will become the edge of town,

nothing but agriculture and one big old tree,
the perfect spot to plant their little four-room home,
to raise a family, add a living room, new bedrooms,
all under the calm, cool shade of the maple.

So of course, we believe this tree will live forever.
We have never known life without its massive trunk,
so big the three of us can't stretch our arms around it,
so rough and yet so comforting, so steadfast in our lives.

The Rope

No one remembers exactly how
we got the rope around the big limb
that stretched out over our roof.
Did we borrow the neighbor's ladder
or tie a brick to the end of the rope
and toss it over? Did we tie a
slip knot and pull it tight like a noose?
Or were we able to straddle the branch
and carefully tie it off like a necktie?
All we remember is the rope, hanging
like a challenge, big knots every few feet
to give a handhold or place to grab on
with your feet while the rope swung below.

At first for us little kids, the rope was just a swing.
Climbing high wasn't an option, but hanging on
to swing out wide across the yard was our thrill.
Then as we each grew, we learned to climb higher.
What a feat it was to reach the top, and how much
braver and stronger we had to be to then grab
the rough fibers of rope that made our fingers red,
get a handhold on the bark, and pull our legs over
onto that sturdy limb. As the youngest, I watched
my siblings and neighbors one by one reach
this milestone, panting, nearly fainting and falling
to the ground, yet gaining access to a peaceful
new world high above the noise of summer lawns.

Sapling

Of course, we believe this tree has lived forever,
despite the fact of the myriad green helicopter seeds
it sends out into the world every spring. We pick them up
to watch them twirl again, dropping them from the roof
when we clean the gutters, sweeping them off the sidewalk,
finding them in the backyard or even blocks away,
a pair of seeds joined at the hip and two light-green
wings, thin filaments and rough veins on either side.

Still, it is impossible to imagine this giant maple
was once a seed, despite what the biology books might say,
and it is impossible to imagine it sprouting from the soil,
like the many tiny stems with mini-maple leaves
we mow every week in early summer. We know
this tree was once a sapling, yet that seems impossible
to wrap our minds around, even as it is impossible
to wrap our arms around its massive trunk today.

A sapling is a supple thing, younger than we are
and as fragile. A sapling bends in the slightest breeze,
and we could break it if we wanted. Its life has been
visible to us from the moment of its sprouting.
But we believe this tree has always been here, longer
than human memory. It has seen more of time than we
will ever live to see, and its silent wisdom is wider
and deeper than we can conceive, so we climb
high in its branches to partake of its cool shade.

A Storm

A few weeks after my mother turned ninety, a storm
blew up the afternoon of a perfect day. The maple
dropped two massive branches, though neither
struck the house. Both fell across the neighbor's
driveway, leaving a gash in the yard but no damage.

In the photos my mother sends, we can tell
they were huge, and though the tree has lost limbs
in the past, these seem bigger, more integral,
and we are simply grateful that no one was hurt,
that the house was spared and the neighbor's car.

Big limbs are down all over town, and crews
come from far away to aid the cleanup. It takes days
before the two branches can be cleared, and it will
be weeks or months before the tree service comes
to inspect the trunk and give their prognosis.

Yet in the photos our neighbor takes, the neighbor
who grew up with us and climbed this tree, we see
the dark, soft pulp in the center of its branches. No wonder
these were the ones lost in the storm. More worrisome:
the same dark, soft cavities high in the old trunk.

A Necessary Lie

We believe a big tree will live forever, though we see the lie.
We have known young trees and watched them die of drought.
We have seen the winds take out branches, even topple
whole trees, tall pines or sturdy oaks, their trunks snapped
like matchsticks or their root balls torn up from soggy ground,
their roots left dangling in the air, clinging to a layer of dirt.

I have seen iris bloom sideways from the ground around
a hackberry's massive clump of roots, hanging on above
a deep hole, the size of a grave, excavated by tornado.
I have seen a tall pecan come crashing down and tear
the roof off a neighbor's house or a live oak level the
back bedroom another neighbor ran from minutes before.

Ice will take down huge limbs in winter, beetles drill holes
to suck the sap and poison the pine's life blood. There is ample
evidence that trees are mortal, yet standing under the big maple,
it was easy to believe it would always be there, until now
when we see its days are numbered: the hollows in its trunk
may be filled, or it may be taken down to save the house.

But we see it could never live forever, as my mother
reminds me that we never know from day to day the span
of our own lives, and I feel like Gilgamesh, after the death
of his great friend, when Utnapishtim, the survivor of the flood,
tells him the gods established death and life, yet humans
cannot know the days of death. For how long do we build a house,

for how long can we sign a lease or raise a child? Every day
we climb that tree. Every day could be its last, and yet we live
as if it isn't. My father died suddenly when his heart gave out,
my sister after seven years of cancer: two gashes in this trunk.
My mother has lost two sisters, a brother, and countless friends
and neighbors, yet she still rises every morning to tend her tree.

The Stump

We want to believe this tree will live forever, but now
that the storm has broached the subject, I have to imagine
a life without its thick, rough bark, without its solid trunk.
A life where its branches are an absence above the roof,
where its shadow is a memory like the sound of dry leaves
on a dry lawn, a time where its tiny helicopter seeds
no longer swirl down from on high every spring.

What will we do when this physical presence no longer
outlives us? What will we do when there is nothing left
but loss, when in place of maple there is only stump?
Will we be here in time to sit and delve into its history,
to examine its many rings, its periods of drought and rain?
Will we count back to find the year my sister was born
or the day my father moved back from Omaha to Iowa?

Will we search for the year my German ancestors
first set foot on the fertile farmland at Deep River or
further back to when this tree was small in a forest, no
fields of corn, no plows or dairy herds? Or will the center
be one dark mass of unknowable time, the rings either
so close on one another like lovers huddling in the cold
or fused or rotted from advanced age and forgetting?

Moon Dog

I can imagine a stump, the remains of the tree
under which I was raised, but can I picture it gone?
What of the night I return in winter to nothing?

No stump, no sign of the tree my parents chose
to build a home beside. No grave except a bare
patch of lawn and a wide expanse of sky.

What of the night when I stand in that yard,
looking for a Pole Star as my guide, and all I see
is an icy crystal ring around a pale, fickle moon?

Yes, the two maples my parents planted
on either side of the driveway will still be there;
young saplings now grown to sentinels

like my brother and I, not giants like the big maple,
but survivors, ready to claim their place,
their branches glistening with frost in moon glow.

Maybe come spring we will plant another
young maple to mark this one's passing. Maybe
it will be the start of a new generation,

but now on this clearest, darkest night,
there is only a moon dog of grief, where once
we climbed rough branches to the stars.

Quarantine

Black Racer

For he seemed to me again like a king,
Like a king in exile, uncrowned in the underworld

      D. H. Lawrence

I still remember coming home to find him
stretched out, lying across our brick steps,
a black snake as long as my leg. I had seen
snakes, even had a run-in with a rattler,
sunning on some rocks in New Mexico,
lethargic enough to ignore our dog and only flick
his tail once we were safely away. I'd been stung,
I thought by wasps in a tall Missouri prairie,
then driven to Texas where my new landlady
pronounced "snakebite" and prescribed Benadryl
when she saw my grapefruit-sized ankle.

So I kept a healthy distance between me
and this king of the ground, though he didn't look
like any venomous creature I could identify
yet was no common garter snake either.
He must have heard my footfall, for soon,
he slithered into our bushes, under the house,
or back into his hole. Later, I read he was more
of a danger to rats and mice than to humans,
and I was glad we had shared a summer morning.

I've never seen another black racer in our yard,
though if he still lives under our porch, I don't mind;
he can have his home and maybe keep rodents away.
I've seen other large snakes on the road or on the path
by the river. I give them a wide berth to pay my respects
to a life that seems both alien and familiar, a life at home
both on and under the ground, not so much deadly
as familiar in the land of the dead, perhaps a messenger
or a reminder that there are limits to our human experience.

Ash Wednesday

for Jane

Olive-green cedar waxwings,
brushed with red tips and black eyeliner,
form a stark contrast against the brilliant
blue morning sky as they feed on berries
in the bare branches of your dogwood.

This after weeks of heavy rain
and dark skies when we haven't
seen you letting the dogs out or
keeping watch over the neighbors
on Fourth Street from your porch.

We don't yet know that you lie
in a hospital bed, that the cancer
has recurred followed by a stroke.
Your daughters haven't told us
you'll be able to come home to die.

How can we know that you will miss
the even darker days to come, the news
of global pandemic and our own social
distancing, when neighbors will only talk
over the fence or wave from the road.

How can we know, in the midst of it all,
the wren will still belt out his love song
from atop a water oak's broken crown
or that fleabane and butterweed
will still bloom in profusion
in every spring ditch and field.

Quarantine

Everything you've ever done has
prepared you for this present moment.
No, prepared isn't right: everything
you've ever done has led you
to this moment, or everything
you've ever done created you
in this moment, or everything
ever done created this moment
with you in suspended animation,
floating in the semi-solid gelatin
of golden memory, surrounded
by all you've done, by windmills
and wheelchairs, bicycles
and binoculars, Camp'otels
and Tilt-a-Whirls, hitchhikers,
hijackers, and holy rollers
speaking in tongues to reveal
that everything that's ever been
has led you to this moment,
endlessly suspended on the
verge of lurching into motion.

Stereoscopic

Earth and sky, mud and water,
blood and breath whirl and swirl.
Here there is primordial ooze
and futuristic sunspot static,
damp canyons and dry arroyos,
hurricanes of magical dust.
Here the eye is a schizophrenic
calm, paradox of paradise in a
dream landscape. Where are
Dali's melting clocks, dripping,
dripping with their semblance
of distorted order? Here the surreal
is natural, normalized, comforting,
yet disturbing. In this stereoscopic
world, there is no more status quo.

Partial Eclipse

I remember I was living in Austin, Texas, as if that matters, when the radio told us, because we still listened to the radio then, where and when the partial solar eclipse could be seen, warned everyone not to look directly at the sun without a dark filter, instructed us how to make a pinhole lens to view on paper or even easier, how to watch the eclipse on the ground by standing in the shade of a tree, and indeed on the sidewalk of my newly rented duplex, hundreds of crescent shadows appeared as if by magic through the gaps in my live oak leaves. I still have the photo I took of this strange apparition. Looking at it now, I still feel the dry summer heat, still feel the hushed silence and simplicity of a time just before the internet, before the pandemic, and I'd like to say before the war, but we had our own wars then, in 1991, in a desert far away, and I had seen wars, mass murders, and epidemics all through my childhood and adolescence, so maybe simplicity is an illusion brought on by the pinhole filter of memory, the dryness, heat, and magic of that moment intensified in many dancing moons.

Zero Gravity

They say the myth of zero gravity can best be explained in free fall,
how the body in orbit, always falling, never landing, remains in free fall.

To approximate zero gravity, astronauts fly to the stratosphere,
sustain a dive long and far enough for them to train in free fall.

Even in the outermost reaches of the universe, black holes and stars tug
a body in all directions; gravity, far from zero, merely aligns in free fall.

Grief feels this weightless, thoughts orbit around the same body, losing
all sense of orientation, down or up, life devolves into a mind in free fall.

Solar systems, even galaxies, all bodies in the universe, orbit or spin
around an axis of gravity, their centripetal forces restrained in free fall.

So, facing the prospect of mortality, ours or our beloved's, the body's
inevitable decline to decomposition, we can but pray to rein in free fall.

Pray grief's dark mountain not cast its shadow long into this bright valley;
pray the sun may rise again after this endless night of rain, in free fall.

Nightshade

The heavy, deadly scent of nightshade hangs
musky-sweet like the smell of the day's first rain.
It pervades the hedgerow where we pull invasive
weeds, bright purple flowers with yellow stamens.

Musky-sweet like the smell of the day's first rain,
the August afternoon hovers in the air, as my love
weeds bright purple flowers with yellow stamens,
deemed deadly poisonous yet eerily beautiful.

The August afternoon hovers in the air as my love
for this place lingers in waves of heat and dry grass.
Deemed deadly poisonous, yet eerily beautiful,
these dark berries entrance whoever beholds them.

For this place lingers in waves of heat and dry grass
even when the season turns to winter and we are far.
These dark berries entrance whoever beholds them,
remaining etched in memory like noxious fumes.

Even when the season turns to winter and we are far,
the heavy deadly scent of nightshade continues to hang,
remaining etched in our memories like the noxious fumes
pervading the hedgerow where now we seem invasive.

Gilgamesh

Grief is a cold dark country
whose citizens are clad in feathers,
whose songs stick in the mouth
like mud and straw drying
in black sun to make bricks.
Here there are no distinctions:
status is leveled, no one holds
power, everyone is masked
and quarantined. Here,
people are no longer people,
but foreigners among their own
kind. Time is irrelevant until
one day you wake to the normal
morning sounds: a dove outside
your window, a car driving by.

Inanna

A flurry of cedar waxwings reveals the mulberry,
its lush fruit nearly ready to ripen into deep, royal
purple. The swallows have returned under the bridges,
crisscrossing air, chasing one another, rebuilding nests,
as one lone drake flies overhead, straight as an arrow.
Pick your goddess: Inanna, Ishtar, Persephone, Astarte.
See her finishing her trek from the underworld, where she
has been replaced by her lover, or her mother has bartered
for her release. Look, the fleabane and wood sorrel signal
her return. The tree canopy is again replete with green,
and the heaviest late winter storms have passed us by.
Yes, there may still be summer hail, even hurricanes.
Yes, we know winter's dark looms just over the horizon.
For now, rejoice in the soft song of her familiar doves.
Rejoice with her bees as they collect sweet nectar.

Orpheus

How do you leave the land of the dead
for which there are no maps or manuals?
Can you walk upright like a man or crawl
on your belly like a worm or a mole?
How can you leave the one you love,
the one whose arms were once bony
and strange, whose cheek turned ever
away from yours? When you arrived here,
everything was dark, lifeless, and cold.
Eventually you fell into that deep,
comforting slumber of familiarity
and forgetting, as your own flesh
grew thin and ethereal and you lay
beside your bride's body, dry and brittle
like the husk of a locust, until you woke
to the sound of heavy rain on the roof,
no, on the earth above, a pounding rain
that seemed to last forever. But now,
the only sound is of sparrows scratching
in the dirt and chirping to one another
signaling the end of the storm and the sun
rising somewhere far, far from here.
Now you remember you were granted
leave for this visit but only under certain
conditions. Now you remember, you must
return to the living, bringing Eurydice.
Yet you already sense her reluctance
and your growing impatience; you already
know you will turn too soon, only to see
her lovely face fade back into the mists,
her face nearly restored to its former
beauty, a face to haunt your final days.

Eurydice

They always make noise, pounding on the hard earth
above with their myriad feet, those strange creatures
you vaguely recall, like ghosts of long-lost relatives.
Yet the man who has come for you claims it is the beating
of life-bringing rain and renewal, a distant memory
of flowers and spring in the relative silence that follows,
and sounds he calls birds. His pleading, musical voice
tugs at your heartstrings, at feelings so dormant
you thought them lost if you could remember at all.
Yours is no desire, no new stirring of life, no will
of your own, and yet as if hypnotized, you follow
those bony heels and the sound of his lyre, upward
through dark passageways most only ever descend.
You warm to the journey, nearly beginning to believe,
until, abruptly, he turns, and you see one final time
his beautiful eyes, his hair and beard glowing in sun.

Osiris

A river is not a coffin: though when
    it floods and wreaks destruction,
        it leaves behind its fertile silt.

A river can cradle a reed boat
    when it carries a baby or your body
        down to Byblos, where

you rock in the warm embrace
    of the salt cedar's tender roots
        as tiny minnows nibble your flesh.

This tree is not a coffin nor a cradle.
    It offers refuge, offers sanctuary,
        takes up your exhausted body

and gives you rest.
    Within its fragrant branches
        you spread sweet shade.

You know, in time, Isis will fell
    this tree to free you, will scatter
        your limbs to the four directions,

will gather strong beams
    to build a temple the dark kite
        will circle, circle, circle.

Isis

hundreds of ibis wading near the shore
    fly up in unison, an eruption
        of water and wing

they rise not in fear but from the desire
    to be airborne, to wade
        through clouds, not waves

to scatter hunger for the beloved
    to the wind, the beloved who is
        fragmented, nearly lost, fading

until they return to settle
    in low green trees that line
        the mouth of the fertile river

In the Beginning,

there was darkness and chaos,
and no one was afraid of the dark
because there was no one. Until
one day Crow appeared and saw
the darkness, and he called it good,
or she called it good because
there were two crows, and no one
knew which came first, the dark
or the crows, and soon there were
so many they were indistinguishable,

until one day someone discovered color,
and songbirds appeared in their midst,
and sunlight came with their songs,
but soon they were hungry, so Crow
created the plants of the fields
and rain to water the plants
and nectar, fruits, and seeds
and schools of fishes in the seas
and worms and reptiles and all
manner of insects for food.

And then, because the crows loved
their creation, they began to experiment,
creating the hairy deer, bears, wolves,
dogs, and other mammals, and strange
creatures like possums, even
the hairless armadillo. Humans
were an afterthought. Truly naked
and pointless. No other animal
would use them for food, and yet
they could mimic bird calls
and were somewhat humorous,
helpless, and pathetic creatures until
they grew up and grew dangerous.

Acknowledgments

I am extremely grateful to the magazines and anthologies that have published versions of poems in this collection:

About Place: "Hidden"

Asahi Haikuist Network: "Crossvine trumpets," "Beside the fountain," and "Mayfly carcasses"

Birmingham Poetry Review: "Partial Eclispe" and "Quarantine"

The Cape Rock: "Spiderwort" and "Patterns"

Delta Poetry Review: "A Different Wind," "Apple Trees," "Ash Wednesday," "Avalon and Ingomar," "Beaver Moon," "Black Racer," "Breathe," "Cancer Root," "Cathedral," "Crow," "Ghost Deer," "Gilgamesh," "Golden Swamp Warbler," "Inanna," "Moon Dog," "Protozoan Transmogrification," "Stereoscopic," and "The Stump"

Ekphrastic Review: "La Llamada (The Call)"

Haiku Page: "Swallows swoop low," "Memory still," and "In the dry ravine"

Juke Joint: "A Necessary Lie"

Peauxdunque Review: "Nightshade" and "Zero Gravity"

Poetry South (edited by Jianqing Zheng): "*Beso con Lengua*" and "Burying the Bed"

Postcard Poems & Prose: "Brethren," "If a bird tweets in the forest," "Passion Flower," and "Poem About the Economy"
River Mouth Revies: "Osiris"
Southern Voices: Fifty Contemporary Poets, Lamar University Literary Press: "*Beso con Lengua*," "Birdsongs," "Cathedral," "Continental Divide," and "Patterns"
Switched-On Gutenberg: "December Flood" and "The Rain in Flanders"
Tar River Poetry: "Birdsongs" and "Deep Freeze"
Texas Review: "November Wind"
Town Creek: "For the record"
Valley Voices: "A tree," "Birthday," "Black Racer," "Continental Divide," "Great Blue," "Heiroglyph," "Making Apple Butter," "One leaf twirls," "Poem," "Tessellations," "Tombigbee River Haiku," "Turning Sixty," "Windfall," and "Windswept Cave"

Many thanks to the Mississippi Arts Commission for the mini-grant and artist fellowship that supported artist residencies at Hambidge Center and Artcroft, where the early poems were composed and revised, and to Lilian Wade and the Mississippi State Committee of the National Museum of Women in the Arts, who first commissioned a poem that turned into the series "Co-evolution," inspired by artists from the National Museum and Mississippi University for Women. I also thank my students and colleagues at The W. I have learned from you and benefitted from our friendships. Thank you to Eric Muhr and the fine staff at Fernwood Press for all they have done to make this book a reality. Finally, my deepest gratitude goes to all my family, especially my mother, Leone Dunkelberg; my wife, Kim Whitehead; and son, Aidan Dunkelberg. Without your love and support, none of this would be possible.

Title Index

A

A blue heron 52
A Different Wind 22
A Necessary Lie 77
A pale full moon 54
Apple Butter 72
Apple Trees 62
Ash Wednesday 82
A Storm 76
A sudden racket 53
A tree 56
Avalon and Ingomar 61
A white egret 52

B

Beaver Moon 36
Beside the fountain 55
Beso con Lengua 25
Birdsong 16
Birthday 69
Black Racer 81

Breathe 45
Brethren 37
Burying the Bed 26

C

Cancer Root 33
Cathedral 42
Continental Divide 34
Crossvine trumpets 55
Crow 19

D

December Flood 23
Deep Freeze 68

E

Eurydice 91

F

For the Record 14

G

Ghost Deer 35
Gilgamesh 88
Great Blue 40

H

Hidden 41
Hieroglyph 20

I

If a Bird Tweets in the Forest 21
Inanna 89
In the Beginning 94
In the dry ravine 57
In the golden sun, men 51
Isis 93

L

La Llamada (The Call) 60
Leafless bushes 54

M

Massive bridge girders 51
Mayfly carcasses 55
Mist on the river 51
Moon Dog 79
Morning sun paints 52

N

Needles 24
Nightshade 87
North Star 66

O

One leaf twirls 57
Orpheus 90
Osiris 92

P

Partial Eclipse 85
Passion Flower 38
Patterns 43
Picking Cherries 71
Poem 39
Poem About the Economy 15
Protozoan Transmogrification 63

Q

Quarantine 83

S

Sapling 75
Sign of spring swallows 53
Spiderwort 32
Splash! 54
Stereoscopic 84
Summer still 56
Swallows swoop low 56

T

Tending Eden 70
Tessellations 28
The Big Maple 73
The Golden Swamp Warbler 30
The Orchard 67
The otter swims 53
The Rain in Flanders 29
The Rope 74
The Stump 78
They Know 18
Three loud kingfishers 57
Turning Sixty 44

W

Windfall 65
Windswept Cave 59

Z

Zero Gravity 86

First Line Index

A

A blue heron 52
A few weeks after my mother turned ninety, a storm 76
A flurry of cedar waxwings reveals the mulberry 89
After Great Aunt Ruth's funeral 26
After the night of heavy storms 42
A kettle of black vultures 37
A mountain or mesa or cliff 59
and there is no other bird to hear it 21
A pale full moon 54
A river is not a coffin: though when 92
As I recall, my imaginary friend's name was John 69
As the sun spills blood 36
A sudden racket 53
A tree 56
A white egret 52

B

Back when I lived in Chicago and still ate meat 25
Be like the great blue heron 40
Beside the fountain 55

C
Crossvine trumpets 55

D
Driving home from Meridian late at night 35

E
Each tree we lost in the orchard would be replaced 67
Earth and sky, mud and water 84
Even in the darkness, there is color 63
Everything you've ever done has 83

F
falls like dark hair across a shoulder 29
feel the air 45

G
Gold coins hang from branches, mist glistening 15
Grief is a cold dark country 88

H
Half the North Star cherry blew down in an autumn storm 65
Here in the orchard 62
How can I say in words what my body 20
How do you leave the land of the dead 90
hundreds of ibis wading near the shore 93

I
I can imagine a stump, the remains of the tree 79
If a drop of rain would fall 34
In the courtyard of stone caryatids 60
In the dark of winter, along frozen canals 28
In the dry ravine 57
In the golden sun, men 51
I remember I was living in Austin, Texas, as if that matters 85
Is it a different wind that blows 22
is officially known as the prothonotary warbler 30
I still remember coming home to find him 81
I've tried to edit you out. After writing you down 24

L

Late June brings a certain warmth in Iowa 71
Leafless bushes 54
Light glances off 61

M

Massive bridge girders 51
Mayfly carcasses 55
Mist on the river 51
Morning sun paints 52

N

No one remembers exactly how 74
No, this is not a crucifix 38
Now that part of the yard is barer, only the grape vines 68

O

Of course, we believe this tree has lived forever 75
Olive-green cedar waxwings 82
One leaf twirls 57

R

Roots burrow in the dark, tunneling through clay 32

S

Sign of spring swallows 53
Splash! 54
Summer still 56
Swallows swoop low 56

T

Take the windfalls, the bruised yet edible 72
The cows know. Standing still 18
The heavy, deadly scent of nightshade hangs 87
The low-hanging boughs of the dwarf apricot 70
The magpie gathers all 16
The murky river surrounds 23
The North Star was a deep red, tart pie cherry 66
The otter swims 53

there was darkness and chaos 94
The tumor takes root, like a seed germinating beneath 33
The water in this stream 39
They always make noise, pounding on the hard earth 91
They say the myth of zero gravity can best be explained in free fall . 86
This morning, a summer 44
This stone holds the pattern 43
Three loud kingfishers 57

W

We believe a big tree will live forever, though we see the lie 77
We believe a tree must live forever 73
We want to believe this tree will live forever, but now 78
When the eye of a cormorant winks at you 14
Winter is the season when hidden beauty 41
Would I were a crow, a dark 19

www.ingramcontent.com/pod-product-compliance
Lightning Source LLC
Chambersburg PA
CBHW010046090426
42735CB00020B/3401

9781594981609